BREAD M.

COOKB

CW00521644

AMERICAN'S FAVOURITE RECIPES

Your Ultimate Guide With Pictures For

Beginners And Advanced Users To Enjoy

Delicious & Healthy Recipes With Every

Bread Maker Including GLUTEN FREE

BAKERY USA

TABLE OF CONTENTS

© *Copyright 2021 by Bakery USA All rights reserved*.

The following Book is reproduced below to provide information that is as accurate and reliable as possible. Regardless, purchasing this Book can be seen as consent to the fact that both the publisher and the author of this book are in no way experts on the topics discussed within and that any recommendations or suggestions that are made herein are for entertainment purposes only. Professionals should be consulted as needed before undertaking any of the actions endorsed herein.

This declaration is deemed fair and valid by both the American Bar Association and the Committee of Publishers Association and is legally binding throughout the United States.

Furthermore, the transmission, duplication, or reproduction of any of the following work including specific information will be considered an illegal act irrespective of if it is done electronically or in print. This extends to creating a secondary or tertiary copy of the work or a recorded copy and is only allowed with the express written consent from the Publisher. All additional rights reserved.

The information in the following pages is broadly considered a truthful and accurate account of facts and as such, any inattention, use, or misuse of the information in question by the reader will render any resulting actions solely under their purview. There are no scenarios in which the publisher or the original author of this work can be in any fashion deemed liable for any hardship or damages that may befall them after undertaking the information described herein.

Additionally, the information in the following pages is intended only for informational purposes and should thus be thought of as universal. As befitting its nature, it is presented without assurance regarding its prolonged validity or interim quality. Trademarks that are mentioned are done without written consent and can in no way be considered an endorsement from the trademark holder.

Overview Of A Bread Machine

A bread machine is more like a small electric oven with a bread tin inside. The bread machine has a kneading paddle that is installed on a waterproof axle and connected to the electric motor at the bottom of the bread tin. This paddle is the one, which has the responsibility to knead the fresh ingredients you load to the bread tin and change them into a smooth and elastic dough.

As you probably have known that making bread requires several steps including ingredients measuring, dough kneading, bread dough proofing, bread dough shaping, and bread baking. Some recipes may also add more steps like glazing the bread and giving bread topping. Because there are so many steps in making bread, it is no secret that making bread takes a long time for the baker without being able to do anything else. Not to mention, the instincts needed to determine whether the dough is good enough or not yet. For some people with lots of time and talent, this process may be interesting. However, for other busy people, this process can be tiring and stressful.

Fortunately, a bread machine comes as a smart solution. Not only kneading, but the bread machine also has functions to do the entire process of making bread. With a bread machine, people have to load the ingredients into the bread tin and let the bread machine shows its magical function. The kneading paddle in the bread tin will spin and knead the ingredients resulting in good dough then the bread machine will let the dough rise and after that, bake the bread. The total time needed for this making bread process may take around 3 or 4 hours. However, the time you have to invest is only not more than 5 minutes. Put the ingredients, touch the buttons, leave the bread machine and come back in a few hours to smell and get tasty bread. It sounds wonderful, doesn't it?

Every different brand of bread machine may offer different menu settings. However, a bread machine has these several cycle settings, depends on what kinds of bread you are going to make.

How To Use A Bread Maker

The processes that occur in a bread machine are not that different than those you use when making bread by hand. They are just less work and mess. The primary techniques used in making bread from a bread machine are:

Mixing and resting.

The ingredients are mixed well and then allowed to rest before kneading. Kneading.

This technique creates long strands of gluten. Kneading squishes, stretches, turns, and presses the dough for 20 to 30 minutes, depending on the machine and setting.

First rise.

This is also called bulk fermentation. Yeast converts the sugar into alcohol, which provides flavor, and carbon dioxide, which provides structure as it inflates the gluten framework.

Stir down (1 and 2).

The paddles rotate to bring the loaf down and redistribute the dough before the second and third rise.

Second and third rise.

The second rise is about 15 minutes. At the end of the third rise, the loaf will almost double in size. Baking. There will be one final growth spurt for the yeast in the dough in the first 5 minutes or so of the baking process, and the bread bakes into the finished loaf. Baking time and temperature will depend on the size, type, and crust setting of the loaf.

Cycles and Settings

Always remember to check the instructions on your bread machine. It varies across different models and types. So, before you start baking, make sure you know how to program your bread machine for the best quality bread. Your bread machine should come with a timing chart for the different types of bread.

There are bread machines that have their weighing scale to ensure a proportionate amount of bread inside the machine. Check the capacity of your bread machine.

The idea of choosing a bread machine can be overwhelming, but most machines have a similar assortment of programmed cycles with precise times and temperatures, so different bread turn out perfectly—or close to perfect. While they may be called slightly different things the most common include:

Basic- This is the most commonly used setting. Often used for traditional white loaves. This setting is what will be used for several savory yeast recipes. This setting should not be used when making sweet bread which can cause over-proofing and will result in overflowing.

Whole Wheat- If you are making bread that uses whole wheat flour, then this is the setting you will use. Whole wheat flour requires a longer bake time. If you use a wheat gluten ingredient, then you may be able to use the basic setting instead. Double-check your user manual to understand which settings is best based on the ingredients you are using.

Gluten-Free- Many of the recipes in this book are gluten-free, so you may find yourself using this setting more than the others. Most of the time the flours used in these recipes act differently than the everyday all-purpose flour or even wheat flour. Many gluten-free recipes will vary slightly or significantly, but most ingredients should be set out and used at room temperature. Many of these bread, although gluten-free, will still require a rise time.

Sweet Bread- This setting is also used often. This setting is what will be used for most sweet bread recipes that include yeast.

French- This setting is what will be used for not just French bread, but different types of artisan bread. When using these settings, you will have bread that comes out with a crispy crust like that of a French or Italian loaf.

Quick/Rapid- This setting may also be labeled either quick cycle or rapid time. This bread will bake quickly and have short rise times. If using a rapid rising yeast, you can sometimes use this setting. To use this setting correctly, consult the user manual of your specific machine to ensure proper use.

Quick Bread- This setting is used for most bread that requires no rising times and can be baked immediately. Banana bread is one example of a recipe you would use this setting for. This setting can also be used to bake cakes in your bread machine as well.

Jam- Some bread machines will offer special settings such as jam. This setting allows you to make your homemade jams.

Dough- This is another specialty setting that some bread machines may offer. The dough setting can be used to make the dough for different pieces of bread, pies crust, and even cookie dough.

Other/Custom- This might include the option to extend baking or rise times by increments, pre-set baking times, or some other function that is explained in your manual.

Different Types Of Bread

Enjoying the best flavors and textures of our baked bread ought to be more than having something to fold around a burger, satisfy your hungry appetite, or satisfying your cravings with excessive empty calories. I'm sure you must have heard about completely abstaining from bread if you want to live the Keto lifestyle, well I am happy to let you know that keto bread can now be an exciting addition to your daily nutritional goals. This is because, unlike your regular bread, keto bread is made with unique ingredients that uphold the law of keto dieting, which is low carbs, high-fat diet predominantly. So if you can't use flour, animal milk, or sugar, does that imply that you'll never have another sandwich or biscuit in your life? No way! Because of the increased demand for gluten-free baked products, there are presently a few distinctive Keto-accommodating ingredient choices accessible, to give you something to toast with your fruits and vegetables for breakfast, lunch, or dinner. Interestingly, these loaves of bread do not taste like the original gluten-free loaves; however, these keto bread and baked goods are quite a delight, as well.

Even though we shall be spending our hard-earned cash on expensive ingredients, it is essential to know where they originate from, what they contribute to our body system, and how they help us. Here are the primary ingredients, and a couple of minors used in Keto bread making:

NATURAL WHEY PROTEIN POWDER

This obviously cannot be described as flour for any reason; however, to make keto bread, it is an incredible substitution. Whey is the fluid that is left after the main phases of cheese production and then processed into a concentrated powder. It is viewed as total protein and contains every one of the nine essential amino acids. Studies have proven that, in addition to improving muscle quality (which helps the muscle to burn more calories), these essential amino acids help avert car-diovascular diseases, diabetes, and age-related bone loss. And there's more from anti-cancer properties to

improving food reaction in kids with asthma. Even though It must be enhanced with our other flours, it breaks down rapidly to help make delectable, healthy, nutrient-rich baked products.

You can find 100% natural unflavored whey protein from health food at online stores, and they are likely to be more affordable than the various brands sold in the grocery stores. It is important to search for products without any additives and also consider the brands and costs while shop-ping.

WHITE BEAN FLOUR

It has a gentle, smooth nutty flavor and braces our shortlist of useable flours in keto bread mak-ing. It contains a one of a kind fiber called resistant starch, which implies that unlike refined carbohydrates that basically melts and blends into our circulatory systems, it goes through the small intestine, for the most part, as undigested fiber. It enhances digestive health by promoting the development of useful microorganisms and manages blood glucose levels because the energy is discharged later in the large intestine, averting sharp spikes and diminishes between meals. Other significant by-products of this flour's digestive process are chemical compounds called "short-chain unsaturated fatty acids," which help counteract colon disease by preventing the ab-sorption of cancer-causing agents (carcinogens). When compared with other flours, it contains the most starches. However, its advantages are more.

COCONUT FLOUR Coconut flour contains about 75% fiber in composition. This is about 9–10 grams for every two tablespoons, which diminishes the absorption of sugar into the circulatory system. It is gotten from pounding the dried white interior meat of the coconut. It is additionally quite tricky to work with and requires consistent practice to get a perfect bread using it, due to its ability to absorb eggs and oil — essentially, anything that is wet—more like an insatiable sponge, absorbing fluids until it is soaked clump of porridge. Hence, it can't be effectively tweaked without altering the fluid ratio of the recipe. This may have a domino impact on the quality and effectiveness of other ingredients in the recipe. It is ideal to follow the recipe precisely until you are comfortable enough to try different things by tweaking the recipes. Coconut flour is certifiably not a critical source of protein in bread recipes but contains lauric acid with antiviral and antifungal properties. Its fragrant, smooth, somewhat sweet nature adds a special component even though small quantities are utilized. It additionally has the awesome nature of fulfilling our hunger cravings for a longer time. Coconut flour is incredibly high in fiber and low in edible carbs. Because it's so high in fiber, it is perfect to be used in preparing weight loss meals.

Research has shown that eating a meal with a quarter cup of coconut flour can diminish caloric stores by as much as 10 percent.

ALMOND FLOUR

Almond flour is purely finely ground whole blanched almonds (without the skin), enriched with essential vitamins and minerals, and high in protein and fiber. Almond meals can be likened to the consistency of cornmeal. Most almond flour brands are more coarsely ground, which influences the final texture in baked products. In thick or brisk-type bread, this doesn't generally make a difference. However, when we're trying to achieve a more tender loaf of white bread, Challah, French-style the appearance and taste response is important. Search for brands that show they are finely ground. They are pricier, but you will be more joyful with the finished product.

GOLDEN FLAXSEED MEAL

Golden flaxseed originates from a delicate wildflower with beautiful, pure, light blue blooms. The fruit is a little pod that contains modest, polished seeds loaded with omega 3 fatty acids, fiber, antioxidants, essential vitamins, and minerals. It is the only flour known to possess zero net carbs (That is, after subtracting the grams of fiber from a similar number of carbohydrates) and has a lot of therapeutic benefits. One exciting discovery I made was that the texture of the bread is significantly improved if the Golden flaxseed meal is further refined in the blender.

At times I come across concerning four potential health issues if a lot of flaxseed meal is consumed. Various studies, in any case, report practically no issues from eating it but rather lists its numerous advantages. Three cyanogenic glycosides contained in flaxseed additionally present in broccoli, kale, and cabbage, among others cease to exist when it is baked. Another study revealed that an individual would need to consume over 8 cups per day to cause toxicity. A large portion of the recipes that include ground flaxseed utilizes just ½ cup for the whole loaf, which can be calculated to be around two tablespoons of flaxseed in two servings.

I accept that too much of any good thing can cause problems. I would likewise not prescribe eating flax seeds wholly, from a nutritional and digestive standpoint. If you would, in any case, rather substitute one of the different flours, you may have the best accomplishment with almond dinner, finely ground. Ground flaxseed is a magnificent wellspring of fundamental supplements and adds a tasty nutty flavor to baked merchandise. Nutritionally both the brilliant and dull as-sortments are the equivalent.

EGG WHITES

Having lots of egg whites in a recipe is genuinely economical and simple to plan. I get them in two different ways; in powder form in a 36-ounce canister that equals 255 egg whites and; in the fluid form, which can be bought with discounts at stores like Costco or 1-quart containers in nearby staple goods. I have seen wide varieties in cost, so be sure to compare before buying. Since they are pasteurized, they won't whip so well as new whites, however adding a small quantity of cream of tartar will make excellent, fluffy steeps similarly as high as using fresh egg whites. Egg whites are essentially 90% water and 10% proteins, which are long chains of amino acids. When we beat air into the whites, these chains become denatured, which implies they unwind and stretch into shapes that trap air, making light textures in what we bake. There is a school of thought that heating/cooking protein which includes protein powders like whey decimates the nutritional worth because our bodies can't assimilate "denatured" foods. This is false. If that were the case, we would need to eat everything raw, right?! Eggs, meat, all that we cook and prepare are denatured when warmed.

The food leaves the stove changed in appearance, yet the protein isn't denatured; rather than being folded into tight molecular balls, the protein chains become long strands.

Cooked or raw, our bodies retain the same essential amino acids. Understanding what denaturing truly is, enables us to appreciate numerous healthy foods, unhindered by senseless arguments.

XANTHAN GUM

No gluten-free flour, or any blend thereof, can copy the flexibility, gas–holding, and binding characteristics of gluten. It does superb, magical things, allowing ease of kneading and stretching, creating superbly chewy, fluffy, and airy bread. Regrettably, it makes a considerable lot of us feel sick. So what are our other options?

Egg whites have been a major help; however, something more is needed to achieve the desired texture and suppleness we're searching for. We have three essential gluten—substitution choices: gums—xanthan and guar; there's also ground seeds like chia and flaxseeds that become gelatinous when water is added, and; unflavored gelatin itself. The bread made with both gelatin and jellied seeds rose and baked well, yet the texture was peculiar — it helped me remember corrugated sheets. A few loaves turned out sticky, and others crumbled a couple of hours later into puckered globs. There might be a winning recipe, but I didn't discover it, and I got tired at some point, reluctant to sentence one more portion to the garbage (I couldn't eat them, even with eggs and veggies). Xanthan can be described as the by-product of a fermentation process as a result of bacteria coming in contact with a sugar source, commonly gotten from corn, wheat, or soy. Numerous individuals on gluten-free diets are hesitant to use it, believing it might contain components of gluten protein. Be that as it may, sugar from whatever source doesn't contain protein.

Xanthan gum is a stunning ingredient as it contains no properties of the sugar it was grown on. If you maintain a strategic distance from it since you think it is a corn or wheat product, it isn't. I might be dwelling on this, yet it is regrettable to dismiss a decent item for proper-ties it doesn't have. Talk about this with your doctor, and if you have second thoughts, you may have much better success with the choices than I did.

STEVIA/SWEETENER

Numerous artificial sweeteners and "sugar-free" items available contain fillers, for example, dextrose or maltodextrin. These can raise glucose the same way as normal sugar. I prefer using 100% stevia powders. The brand I use is Kal. I additionally love using EZ Sweetz drops as it appears to me to have the least bitter lingering flavor; however, do go for your favorite brand. Every brand has its preferred units of measurements: teaspoons, drops, a bundle, or a small scoop, so be sure to check the label and use the appropriate measurements.
HONEY

Honey is important to give food to the yeast being used since the flours used in the keto diet don't contain sugars to eat or starches to convert into glucose. You can use ordinary sugar if you like; just one tablespoon is used for the Nutrition and separated into 8, 12, or 16 servings, our portion is quite small. According to the American Diabetes Association, consuming white sugar increases blood glucose levels somewhat quicker than Honey, which has a glycemic run somewhere in the range of 31 and 78 relying upon the variety.

Locust honey, for example, has a glycemic index (GI) of 32; clover honey has 69. You can investigate this further on online sites like the Glycemic Index Database. Local raw nectar additionally seems to help regular sensitivities since the honey bees gather region dust, which helps construct your invulnerability.

COCONUT OIL

There is a wide range of health benefits obtained from coconut oil. It's beneficial for your heart, your assimilation, and your resistant framework, and is additionally valuable in assisting with weight reduction. It has a light, however particular coconut flavor.

ALMOND BUTTER

Almonds top the chart of the "world's most beneficial foods" list on the earth. Almond butter gives a pleasant nutty flavor, which can be likened to peanut spread in your dishes.

CASHEW BUTTER

Rich in a few distinct nutrients, cashew butter is additionally high in protein and is a great substitute for butter or nutty spread in a recipe. It does have an aftertaste like cashews.

MACADAMIA BUTTER

Macadamia nuts are a rich source of dietary fiber and monounsaturated fats. The butter is sweet and velvety and lessens bad cholesterol in the body while increasing good cholesterol. Macadamia butter is a good substitution for regular butter and has a sweet, nutty flavor.

ALMOND MILK

Pressed from almond seeds, almond milk is high in protein and low in bad fats. It's a perfect, tasty swap for dairy and has a scarcely recognizable and very mellow flavor.

COCONUT MILK

Pressed from the meat of the coconut, coconut milk keeps up stable glucose and advances cardiovascular, bone, muscle, and nerve wellbeing. It gives a rich, sweet coconut flavor to your dishes.

YEAST

I buy ACTIVE dry yeast in economical 2-pound bundles and store it in a zip lock bag in the freezer. It just takes two or three minutes for one tablespoon of yeast powder to warm to room temperature. I measure it straight from the freezer, (speedily returning it), regularly adding it to the bowl of dry ingredients without proofing (allowing it to break down and activate it into a froth before adding to the batter).

Yeast production today is very reliable. Proofing is only useful if it is past the expiry date, and you have to test whether it is still good and can be useful. It will activate when it interacts with the fluid fixings in the blending procedure. There is just one rise withlow-carb bread. This is my hypothesis, though, however, since yeast has so little to eat—essentially only a tablespoon of Honey I don't

need it to generate the entirety of its energy in a different dish; I need its work to begin inside the batter. I tried this, one loaf with sealed yeast included and the other with the yeast entering the batter dry; the subsequent loaf rose higher. All brand name names of yeast sold in North America are without gluten except for brewer's yeast utilized in a larger production.

DIASTATIC MALT POWDER

Diastatic Malt Powder has, for some time, been a hidden secret of professional bakers. Albeit just one teaspoon is added to every one of the following recipes, it critically enhances the flavor and produces an appetizing home-baked bread aroma. It is listed as a discretionary element for gluten-free diets since it is produced from sprouted grains (for example, barley) that have been dried and ground. Luckily gluten-free varieties of malt and malt substitutes are additionally being created and are accessible on a limited basis. "Diastatic" alludes to the enzymes that are present as the grain newly sprouts, which convert starches into sugars and advances yeast growth.

I have not been able to decide whether these enzymes separate the resistant starches found in white bean flour; I just know the taste and texture are better, and the bread remains fresh for a more extended period. It usually comes in a 1-pound pack that is generally cheap because only one teaspoon is utilized per portion. Note: Do not mistake this for non–diastatic, which is a sugar without any enzymes.

MEATS AND PROTEINS

Your meats need to come from grass-fed, organically produced livestock, free-range poultry, or wild-caught fish and assorted types of seafood. Wild game is excellent, as well, in case you're so interested. Meats, for example, venison, are very low in bad fats while high in good fats and lean protein, so don't hesitate to get some for yourself!

Overview Of Ketogenic Diet

The ketogenic diet or the keto diet, as it is popularly known, is a diet that is mainly characterized by its low-carbohydrate content, with more focus on having high-protein content and high-fat food Ingredients, as well. Having a lower carbohydrate intake enables the body to break down fat easily, which, in turn, results in the production of ketone bodies. The main and most popular use of the keto diet among users is for weight loss.

Our bodies are dependent on glucose produced from the breakdown of carbohydrates to function and have energy. In a keto diet, glucose is replaced by ketone bodies, which are a result of breaking down fat instead. The number of ketone bodies in the body can be measured using blood or urine samples to ensure the body remains in a state of ketosis.

Some notable health benefits of the keto diet are weight loss and reduced amount of blood sugar levels in the body, among others. These are the results of taking fewer carbohydrates in your diet.

The Keto diet emphasizes more on healthy protein and fat. Fat, in this case, means saturated and monosaturated fat, which are beneficial to the body and not unhealthy at all. The keto diet also emphasizes the consumption of whole foods, as well as food that is fresh, including fresh meats, eggs, vegetables, and fruits, while reducing the intake of processed foods. This makes it easy to do in the long run because it only calls for the reduction of one type of food but not completely cutting it off.

For our bodies to function well, we need a whole group of nutrients to do so. What we, therefore, consume at the end of the day must be able to meet these needs. The nutrients you consume are divided into two essential groups, namely macronutrients and micronutrients. Macronutrients are, for example, carbohydrates, proteins, and fats, while micronutrients are minerals and vitamins found in the food we eat.

Keto And Gluten

Gluten is a protein found in wheat and grains that enhances ground flour's elasticity and causes them to rise (proof). The Latin word for gluten is "glue." It's additionally the binding component that gives bread its chewy texture and prevents it from crumbling after the baking process. Glu-ten can be separated from flour because it is insoluble in water. Ordinarily, when you remove the gluten factor in these flours, you additionally lose the fantastic properties that make bread and cakes what they are. Without gluten, your baked products won't rise, and they'll have a grainy, crumbly texture. They won't taste anything like their gluten-loaded cousins, and you presumably won't have any desire to eat more than the first nibble. Given the increased interest in gluten-free foods, food companies have devoted a tremendous measure of time and cash into making scrumptious, lasting, gluten-free products. Regrettably, most commercially manufactured gluten-free bread and cake mixes still fall short of actually being "gluten-free"!

Is the Keto/Paleo Diet Gluten-Free?

Since gluten is mostly present in wheat and grains, the Keto diet is gluten-free. All grain items are termed forbidden in the Keto/Paleo world. Keep in mind, the original creator of the Paleo diet was a gastroenterologist who was creating a meal plan that would assist his patients suffering from gastric disorders. Gluten intolerance is one of the most predominant causes of gastrointestinal diseases in Western civilization

What Is Gluten Intolerance?

Gluten intolerance, or celiac sickness in its advanced stages, is a condition that destroys the cells the small intestine. It is usually activated by eating foods that have gluten in them. A portion of such foods include:

- Cookies

- Pretty much any baked products

- Most flours, including white and wheat flours

- Pizza dough

Gluten triggers an autoimmune reaction in the small intestine that causes problems within the or-gan. This can prompt an inability to absorb important nutrients from the digestive tract. Other ailments related to this disease include lactose intolerance, bone loss, several types of cancerous growth, neurological complications, and malnutrition. Illnesses notwithstanding, only the side effects of gluten intolerance can disrupt your everyday life.

They include:

- Weakness
- Joint pain
- Depression
- Neurological disorders Severe diarrhea
- Stomach cramps
- Intestinal inflammation
- Joint torment
- Bone diseases
- Rashes

These are just a few of the manifestations that an individual with gluten intolerance can experience, and as a result, all foods that contain gluten are prohibited on the Keto/Paleo diet plan. Now, you can see the reason why this diet has triggered a lot of interest. The Harmful Effects of Gluten on our foods

Gluten doesn't simply hurt individuals with end stages of celiac diseases. It is destructive to every one of us, and it is only a matter of time before we see the harmful results. A good number of researches have shown that individuals who have even a mild sensitivity to gluten display a significantly higher risk of death than individuals who don't. The awful part is that 99 percent of individuals with gluten sensitivity don't realize they have it. They credit their side effects to different conditions, for example, stress or fatigue.

Garlic, herb and cheese bread

Preparation Time: 5 minutes **Cooking Time**: 45 minutes **Serving**: 12

Ingredients:

- cup ghee
- eggs
- cups almond flour
- tsp baking powder
- tsp xanthan gum
- cup cheddar cheese, shredded
- tbsp garlic powder
- tbsp parsley
- tbsp. oregano
- tsp salt

Directions:

1.   Lightly beat eggs and ghee before pouring into the bread machine pan.

2. Add the remaining ingredients to the pan.

3.   Set the bread machine to gluten-free.

4.   When the bread is done, remove the bread machine pan from the bread machine. 5.Let cool slightly before transferring to a cooling rack.

6.You can store your bread for up to 5 days in the refrigerator.

Nutrition:

Calories 156

Carbohydrates 4 g Fats 13 g Sugar 4g Protein 5 g

Garlic Bread

Preparation time: 2 hours **Cooking Time**: 15 minutes **Servings**: 6

Ingredients:

5 oz beef

15 oz almond flour

5 oz rye flour

1 onion

3   teaspoons dry yeast

5 tablespoons olive oil

1 tablespoon sugar

 Sea salt

Ground black pepper

Directions:

Pour the warm water into the 15 oz of the wheat flour and rye flour and leave overnight. Chop the onions and cut the beef into cubes.

Fry the onions until clear and golden brown and then mix in the bacon and fry on low heat for 20 minutes until soft.

Combine the yeast with the warm water, mixing until smooth consistency, and then combine the yeast with the flour, salt and sugar, but don't forget to mix and knead well.

Add in the fried onions with the beef and black pepper and mix well.

Pour some oil into a bread machine and place the dough into the bread maker. Cover the dough with the towel and leave for 1 hour.

Close the lid and turn the bread machine on the basic/white bread program.

Bake the bread until the medium crust and after the bread is ready take it out and leave for 1 hour covered with the towel and only then you can slice the bread.

Nutrition:

carbo-hydrates 6

g

fats 21 g

protein 13 g

calories 299

Egg bread

Preparation time: 15 minutes **Cooking Time**: 3 hours **Servings**: 8

Ingredients:

4   cups almond flour 1 cup milk

2 eggs

1 teaspoon yeast

1   ½ teaspoons salt

2   ¼ tablespoons sugar 1 ½ tablespoons butter

Directions:

Lay the products in the bread pan according to the instructions for your device. At me in the beginning liquid, therefore we pour warm milk, and we will add salt. Then add the eggs (preloosen with a fork) and melted butter, which must be cooled to a warm state.

Now add the sifted almond flour.

Top the yeast - dry active ones, since they do not require preactivation with liquid. In the end, mix the yeast with sugar.

Select the basic program (on mine, it is 1 of 12). The time will automatically be set for 3 hours. When the batch begins, this is the most crucial moment. Kneading on this program lasts precisely 10 minutes, from which a ball of all products is produced. Not porridge, not liquid, not a rough dense lump – namely a softball.

Ideally, it is formed after the first 4-5 minutes of kneading; then you can help the bread maker. First, scrape off the flour from the walls, which the blade sometimes does not entirely grasp and thus interferes with the dough. Second, you need to look carefully, as different flours from different manufacturers have different degrees of humidity, so it may take a little more - about 2-3 tablespoons. This is when you see that the dough cannot condense and gather in a ball.

Very rarely, but sometimes it happens that there is not enough liquid and the dough turns into lumps. If so, add a little more water and thereby help the bread maker knead the dough.

After exactly 3 hours, you will hear the signal, but much sooner, your home will be filled with the fantastic aroma of homemade bread. Turn off the appliance, open the lid, and take out the bowl of bread. Handsome!

Take out the hot egg bread, and remove the paddle if it does not stay in the bowl, but is at the bottom of the loaf. Cool the loaves on a grate. In general, it is always advised to cool the bread on its side.
This bread is quite tall - 12 cm.

Only when the loaf completely cools, you can cut the egg bread! Help yourself!

Nutrition: Carbohydrates 3 g
fats 5.6 g protein 9.6 g calories 319

Simple keto bread

Preparation time: 3 minutes ***Cooking Time***: 15 minutes ***Servings***: 8

Ingredients:

3   cups almond flour 2 tbsp inulin

1   tbsp whole milk

½ tsp salt

2   tsp active yeast

1 ¼ cups warm water 1 tbsp olive oil

Directions:

Use a small mixing bowl to combine all dry ingredients, except for the yeast. In the bread machine pan add all wet ingredients.

Add all of your dry ingredients, from the small mixing bowl to the bread machine pan. Top with the yeast. Set the bread machine to the basic bread setting. When the bread is done, remove the bread machine pan from the bread machine. Let cool slightly before transferring to a cooling rack. The bread can be stored for up to 5 days on the counter and up to 3 months in the freezer.

Nutrition: carbohydrates 4 g fats 7 g protein 3 g calories 85

Healthy spiced cauliflower buns

Total time: 40 minutes **Preparation time**: 10 minutes **Cooking time**: 30 minutes **Serving**: 8

Ingredients:
- 2 tablespoons coconut flour
- 1 tablespoon olive oil
- 1/4 teaspoon ground turmeric
- 2 cups chopped cauliflower
- 2 eggs
- A pinch each of salt & pepper

Directions:

preheat your oven to 400 degrees. Prepare a loaf pan by lining with parchment paper and greasing with cooking spray.

Process cauliflower in a food processor into 'rice'; steam the cauliflower rice until tender.

Transfer the steamed cauliflower to a bowl and mix in turmeric, eggs, olive oil, salt, and pepper until well blended; form buns from the mixture and arrange them onto a baking sheet. Bake for about 30 minutes or until light brown, serve hot.

Nutrition: calories: 187; total fat: 9.1 g; carbs: 6.6 g; dietary fiber: 9 g; sugars: 2.4 g; protein: 4.5 g;

Pumpkin and sunflower seed bread

Preparation Time: 8 minutes **Cooking Time**: 15 minutes **Serving**: 10

Ingredients:

- cup ground psyllium husk
- cup chia seeds
- cup pumpkin seeds
- cup sunflower seeds
- tbsp ground flaxseed
- tsp baking soda
- tsp salt
- tbsp coconut oil, melted
- ¼ cup egg whites
- cup almond milk

Directions:

1.   Place all wet ingredients into the bread machine pan first. 2.Add dry ingredients.

3.   Set the bread machine to the gluten-free setting.

4.   When the bread is done, remove the bread machine pan from the bread machine.

5.   Let cool slightly before transferring to a cooling rack.

6.   You can store your bread for up to 5 days in the refrigerator.

Nutrition:

Calories 155

Carbohydrates 4 g

Fats 8 g

Sugar 3g   Protein 5 g

Low-Carb Cauliflower Bread

Preparation Time: 20 minutes **Cooking Time**: 45 min **Serving**: 8

Ingredients:

- 2 cups almond flour
- 5 eggs
- ¼ cup psyllium husk 1 cup cauliflower rice

Directions:

Preheat broiler to 350 ºF.

Line a portion skillet with material paper or coconut oil cooking shower. Put in a safe spot.

In an enormous bowl or nourishment processor, blend the almond flour and psyllium husk.

Beat in the eggs on high for as long as two minutes.

Blend in the cauliflower rice and mix well.

Empty the cauliflower blend into the portion skillet.

Heat for as long as 55 minutes.

Nutrition: 398 Calories; 21g Fat; 4.7g Carbs; 44.2g Protein; 0 .5g Sugars

Rosemary & Garlic Coconut Flour Bread

Preparation Time: 20 minutes **Cooking Time**: 45 min

Ingredients:

- 1/2 cup Coconut flour
- 1 stick margarine (8 tbsp)
- 6 enormous eggs
- 1 tsp Heating powder 2 tsp Dried Rose-mary
- 1/2-1 tsp garlic powder 1/2 tsp Onion powder
- 1/4 tsp Pink Himalayan Salt

Directions:

Join dry fixings (coconut flour, heating powder, onion, garlic, rosemary, and salt) in a bowl and put in a safe spot.

Add 6 eggs to a different bowl and beat with a hand blender until you get see rises at the top.

Soften the stick of margarine in the microwave and gradually add it to the eggs as you beat with the hand blender.

When wet and dry fixings are completely consolidated in isolated dishes, gradually add the dry fixings to the wet fixings as you blend in with the hand blender.

Oil an 8x4 portion dish and empty the blend into it equitably.

Heat at 350 for 40-50 minutes (time will change contingent upon your broiler).

Let it rest for 10 minutes before expelling from the container. Cut up and appreciate it with spread or toasted!

Nutrition: 398 Calories; 21g Fat; 4.7g Carbs; 44.2g Protein; 0.5g Sugars

Best Keto Garlic Bread

Preparation Time: 10

Cooking Time: 15

Ingredients:

- Garlic and Herb Compound Butter:
- 1/2 cup mellowed unsalted margarine (113 g/4 oz)   1/2 tsp salt (I like pink Himalayan salt)
- 1/4 tsp ground dark pepper
- 2 tbsp additional virgin olive oil (30 ml)
- 4 cloves garlic, squashed
- 2 tbsp naturally slashed parsley or 2 tsp dried parsley

Topping:

1/2 cup ground Parmesan cheddar (45 g/1.6 oz) 2 tbsp crisp parsley

Discretionary: sprinkle with additional virgin olive oil

Alternative options:

Extreme Keto Buns Nut-Free Keto Buns

Psyllium-Free Keto Buns Flax-Free Keto Bread

Directions:

Set up the keto sourdough rolls by following this formula (you can make 8 standard or 16 smaller than usual loaves). The Best Low-Carb Garlic Bread

Set up the garlic margarine (or some other seasoned spread). Ensure every one of the fixings has arrived at room temperature before blending them in a medium bowl. The Best Low-Carb Garlic Bread

Cut the prepared rolls down the middle and spread the enhanced margarine over every half (1-2 tea-spoons for each piece). The Best Low-Carb Garlic Bread

Sprinkle with ground Parmesan and spot back in the stove to fresh up for a couple of more minutes. The Best Low-Carb Garlic Bread

At the point when done, expel from the stove. Alternatively, sprinkle with some olive oil and serve while still warm.

Nutrition: calories 270, fat 15, fiber 3, carbs 5, protein 9

Low Carb Flax Bread

Preparation Time: 10 minutes ***Cooking Time***: 24 min ***Serving***: 8

Ingredients:

- 200 g ground flax seeds
- ½ cup psyllium husk powder 1 tablespoon heating powder 1 ½ cups soy protein separate
- ¼ cup granulated Ste-via 2 teaspoons salt
- 7 enormous egg whites 1 enormous en-tire egg
- 3 tablespoons margarine
- ¾ cup water

Directions:

Preheat broiler to 350 degrees F.

Mix psyllium husk, heating powder, protein disengage, sugar, and salt in a bowl.

In a different bowl, blend egg, egg whites, margarine, and water. On the off chance that you are including concentrates or syrups, include them here.
Slowly add wet fixings to dry fixings and consolidate.

Grease your bread dish with a spread or splash.

Add the blend to the bread dish

Bake 15-20 minutes until set.
Nutrition:
Cal: 20,
Carbs: 5g/
Net Carbs: 5.5 g, Fiber:8.5 g,
Fat: 13 g, Protein: 10g, Sugars: 5 g.

Low Carb Focaccia Bread

Preparation Time: 10 minutes **Cooking Time**: 25 min **Serving**: 12

Ingredients:

- 1 cup almond flour 1 cup flaxseed feast
- 7 enormous eggs
- ¼ cup olive oil
- 1 ½ tablespoons heating pow-der
- 2 teaspoons minced garlic

- 1 teaspoon salt
- 1 teaspoon rosemary
- 1 teaspoon red bean stew chips

Directions:

Preheat your broiler to 350F.

In a blending bowl, join all your dry fixings and blend well.

Start including your garlic and 2 eggs one after another, blending in with a hand blender to get a mixture sort of consistency.

Add your olive oil last, blending it well until everything is joined. The more aerated the hitter turns into, the more "cushy" your bread will turn into.

Put every one of your fixings into a lubed 9x9 heating dish, smooth out with a spatula.

Bake for 25 minutes.

Let cool for 10 minutes and expel from the lubed heating dish.

Cut into squares and cut the squares down the middle. Add whatever you'd prefer to the center!

Nutrition:

Cal: 50, Carbs: 4g/ Net Carbs: 2.5 g, Fiber:4.5 g, Fat: 8 g, Protein: 8g, Sugars: 3 g.

Lemon & Rosemary Low Carb Shortbread

Preparation Time: 5 minutes **Cooking Time**: 20 min **Serving**: 6

Ingredients:

- 6 tablespoons margarine 2 cups almond flour
- 1/3 cup granulated Splenda (or other granulated sugar) 1 tablespoon naturally ground lemon get-up-and-go
- 4 teaspoons crisp pressed lemon juice
- 1 teaspoon vanilla concentrate
- 2 teaspoons rosemary*
- ½ teaspoon preparing pop

- ½ teaspoon preparing powder

Directions:

In a huge blending bowl, measure out 2 cups of almond flour, 1/2 tsp. heating powder and 1/2 tsp. preparing pop. Include 1/3 cup Splenda, or another granulated sugar blend. Put in a safe spot.

Zest your lemon with a Microplane until you have 1 Tbsp. lemon get-up-and-go. Squeeze a large portion of the lemon to get 4tsp lemon juice.

In the microwave, liquefy 6 Tbsp. of margarine and afterward include 1 tsp. vanilla concentrate.

Transfer your almond flour and sugar to a little blending bowl. Put your spread, lemon get up and go, lemon squeeze, and slashed rosemary into the now vacant huge blending bowl. Include your almond flour once more into the wet blend gradually, mixing as you go. Continue blending until all the almond flour is included back.

Wrap the mixture firmly in cling wrap.

Place the enveloped batter by the cooler for 30 minutes, or until hard.

Preheat your stove to 350F, evacuate your batter, and unwrap it.

Cut your batter in ~1/2" increases with a sharp blade. this blade isn't sharp, it will cause the batter to disintegrate. On the off chance that the mixture is as yet disintegrating, that implies it needs additional time in the cooler.

Grease a treat sheet with SALTED margarine and spot your treats onto it.

Nutrition Cal: 100, Carbs: 2g/ Net Carbs: 5.5 g, Fiber:4.5 g, Fat: 10 g, Protein: 2g, Sugars: 4 g.

Low-Carb Garlic & Herb Focaccia Bread

Preparation Time: 10 minutes

Cooking Time: 25 min

Serving: 7

Ingredients:

- cup Almond Flour
- ¼ cup Coconut Flour
- ½ teaspoon Xanthan Gum
- 1 teaspoon Garlic Powder
- 1 teaspoon Flaky Salt
- ½ teaspoon Heating Soda
- ½ teaspoon Heating Powder Wet Ingredients

- eggs
- teaspoon Lemon Juice
- teaspoon Olive oil + 2 teaspoons of Olive Oil to sprinkle Top with Italian Seasoning and TONS of flaky salt!

Directions:

Heat broiler to 350 and line a preparing plate or 8-inch round dish with the material.

Whisk together the dry fixings ensuring there are no knots.

Beat the egg, lemon squeeze, and oil until joined.

Mix the wet and the dry, working rapidly, and scoop the mixture into your dish.

Make sure not to blend the wet and dry until you are prepared to place the bread in the broiler because the raising response starts once it is blended!!!

Smooth the top and edges with a spatula dunked in water (or your hands) at that point utilize your finger to dimple the batter. Try not to be hesitant to dive deep into the dimples! Once more, a little water prevents it from staying.

Bake secured for around 10 minutes. Sprinkle with Olive Oil heat for an extra 10-15 minutes revealing to dark-colored tenderly.

Top with increasingly flaky salt, olive oil (discretionary), a scramble of Italian flavoring and crisp basil. Let cool totally before cutting for an ideal surface!!

Nutrition: Cal: 80,

Carbs: 16g

Net Carbs: 2.5 g, Fiber:8.5 g,

Fat: 7 g, Protein: 8g, Sugars: 10 g.

Cauliflower Bread with Garlic & Herbs

Preparation Time: 9 minutes **Cooking Time**: 26 min **Serving**: 12

Ingredients:

3   cup Cauliflower ("riced" utilizing nourishment processor*)

10 enormous Egg (isolated)

1/4 teaspoon Cream of tartar (discretionary)

1 1/4 cup Coconut flour

1 1/2 teaspoon sans gluten heating pow-der

1 teaspoon Sea salt

6 teaspoon Butter (unsalted, estimated strong, at that point softened; can utilize ghee for sans dairy) 6 cloves Garlic (minced)

1 teaspoon Fresh Rosemary (slashed) 1 teaspoon Fresh parsley (slashed) Direction:

Preheat the broiler to 350 degrees F (177 degrees C). Line a 9x5 in (23x13 cm) portion skillet with material paper.

Steam the riced cauliflower. You can do this in the microwave (cooked for 3-4 minutes, shrouded in plastic) OR in a steamer bin over water on the stove (line with cheesecloth if the openings in the steamer containers are too huge, and steam for a couple of moments). The two different ways, steam until the cauliflower is delicate and delicate. Enable the cauliflower to sufficiently cool to deal with. Meanwhile, utilize a hand blender to beat the egg whites and cream of tartar until solid pinnacles structure.

Place the coconut flour, preparing powder, ocean salt, egg yolks, dissolved margarine, garlic, and 1/4 of the whipped egg whites in a nourishment processor. When the cauliflower has cooled enough to deal with, envelop it by kitchen towel and press a few times to discharge however much dampness as could reasonably be expected. (This is significant - the final product ought to be dry and bunch together.) Add the cauliflower to the nourishment processor. Procedure until all-around joined. (Blend will be thick and somewhat brittle.)

Add the rest of the egg whites to the nourishment processor. Overlay in only a bit, to make it simpler to process. Heartbeat a couple of times until simply consolidated. (Blend will be cushioned.) Fold in the hacked parsley and rosemary. (Don't over-blend to abstain from separating the egg whites excessively.) Transfer the player into the lined heating skillet. Smooth the top and adjust somewhat. When-ever wanted, you can squeeze more herbs into the top (discretionary).

Bake for around 45-50 minutes, until the top, is brilliant. Cool totally before expelling and cutting.

How To Make Buttered Low Carb Garlic Bread

(discretionary): Top cuts liberally with spread, minced garlic, crisp parsley, and a little ocean salt. Prepare in a preheated stove at 450 degrees F (233 degrees C) for around 10 minutes. On the off chance that you need it progressively sautéed, place under the oven for several minutes.

Nutrition Cal: 70,

Carbs: 4g/ Net Carbs: 2.5 g, Fiber:4.5 g, Fat: 15 g, Protein: 4g, Sugars: 3 g.

Grain-Free Tortillas Bread

Preparation Time: 5 minutes ***Cooking Time:*** 20 min ***Serving***: 5

Ingredients:

96 g almond flour

24 g coconut flour

2 teaspoons thickener

1   teaspoon heating pow-der 1/4 teaspoon fit salt

2   teaspoons apple juice vinegar 1 egg softly beaten

3   teaspoons wanted

Directions:

Add almond flour, coconut flour, thickener, preparing powder, and salt to nourishment processor. Heartbeat until completely joined. Note: you can, on the other hand, whisk everything in a huge bowl and utilize a hand or stand blender for the accompanying advances.

Pour in apple juice vinegar with the nourishment processor running. When it has dispersed equally, pour in the egg. Pursued by the water. Stop the nourishment processor once the batter structures into a ball. The batter will be clingy to contact.

Wrap mixture in stick film and ply it through the plastic for a moment or two. Consider it somewhat like a pressure ball. Enable the mixture to rest for 10 minutes (and as long as three days in the refrigerator).

Heat up a skillet (ideally) or container over medium warmth. You can test the warmth by sprinkling a couple of water beads if the drops vanish promptly your dish is excessively hot. The beads should 'go' through the skillet.

Break the mixture into eight 1" balls (26g each). Turn out between two sheets of material or waxed paper with a moving pin or utilizing a tortilla press (simpler!) until each round is 5-crawls in distance across.

Transfer to skillet and cook over medium warmth for only 3-6 seconds (significant). Flip it over promptly (utilizing a meager spatula or blade), and keep on cooking until just daintily brilliant on each side (however with the customary roasted imprints), 30 to 40 seconds. The key is-n't to overcook them, as they will never again be flexible or puff up.

Keep them warm enclosed by kitchen fabric until serving. To rewarm, heat quickly on the two sides, until simply warm (not exactly a moment).

These tortillas are best destroyed straight. Be that as it may, don't hesitate to keep some mixture convenient in your ice chest for as long as three days, and they likewise freeze well for as long as a quarter of a year.

Nutrition Cal: 70,

Carbs: 22g

Net Carbs: 2.5 g, Fiber:4.5 g, Fat: 8 g, Protein: 8g, Sugars: 3 g.

Cauliflower Tortillas Bread

Preparation Time: 6 minutes

Cooking Time: 21 min

Serving: 5

Ingredients:

- 3/4 huge head cauliflower (or two cups riced)
- 2 huge eggs (Vegans, sub flax eggs)
- 1/4 cup cleaved crisp cilantro
- 1/2 medium lime, squeezed and zest-ed salt and pepper, to taste

Directions:

Preheat the stove to 375 degrees F., and line a heating sheet with material paper.

Trim the cauliflower cut it into little, uniform pieces, and heartbeat in a nourishment processor in groups until you get a couscous-like consistency. The finely riced cauliflower should make around 2 cups pressed.

Place the cauliflower in a microwave-safe bowl and microwave for 2 minutes, at that point mix and microwave again for an additional 2 minutes. If you don't utilize a micro-wave, a steamer works similarly also. Spot the cauliflower in a fine cheesecloth or slender dish-towel and crush out however much fluid as could be expected, being mindful so as not to consume yourself. Dishwashing gloves are recommended as it is exceptionally hot.

In a medium bowl, whisk the eggs. Include cauliflower, cilantro, lime, salt, and pepper. Blend until all around consolidated. Utilize your hands to shape 6 little "tortillas" on the material paper.

Bake for 10 minutes, cautiously flip every tortilla and come back to the stove for an extra 5 to 7 minutes, or until totally set. Spot tortillas on a wire rack to cool marginally.

Heat a medium-sized skillet on medium. Spot a prepared tortilla in the container, pushing down somewhat, and dark-colored for 1 to 2 minutes on each side. Rehash with residual tortillas.

Nutrition Cal: 30,

Carbs: 8g/

Net Carbs: 2.5 g, Fiber: 7.5 g, Fat: 8 g, Protein: 10g,

Herb Focaccia Bread

Preparation Time: 3.5 hours **Cooking Time**: 45 minutes **Servings**: 8

Difficulty: Expert

Ingredients:

- Dough:
- cup water
- tablespoons canola oil
- teaspoon salt
- teaspoon dried basil
- cups bread flour
- teaspoons bread machine yeast
  Topping:
- tablespoon canola oil
- cup fresh basil
- cloves garlic (to taste)
- tablespoons grated parmesan cheese
- pinch salt
- tablespoon cornmeal (option-

Directions:1.   Put all of the bread ingredients in your bread machine, in the order listed above starting with the water, and finishing with the yeast. Make a well in the middle of the flour and place the yeast in the well. Make sure the well doesn't touch any liquid. Set the bread machine to the dough function.

2. Check on the dough after about 5 minutes and make sure that it's a softball. Add water 1 tablespoon at a time if it's too dry, and add flour 1 tablespoon at a time if it's too wet.

3. When the dough is ready put it on a lightly floured hard surface. Cover the dough and let it rest for 10 minutes.

4. While the dough is resting, chop up the garlic and basil, grease a 13x9 inch pan and evenly distribute cornmeal on top of it.

5. Once the dough has rested, press it into the greased pan. Drizzle oil on the dough and evenly distribute the salt parmesan, garlic, and basil.

Nutrition:

Calories: 108 Carbs: 37.4 g Fiber: 1.6 g Fat: 7.3 g Protein: 7.7 g.Chapter 9. Cheese Loaves

Cheese Blend Bread

Preparation Time: 25 minutes **Cooking Time**: 15 minutes **Serving**: 12

Ingredients:

- oz. cream cheese
- cup ghee
- 2/3 cup almond flour
- cup coconut flour
- tbsps. whey protein, unflavored
- tsp baking powder
- tsp Himalayan salt
- cup parmesan cheese, shredded
- tbsps. water
- eggs
- cup mozzarella cheese, shredded

Directions:

1. Place wet ingredients into bread machine pan.

2. Add dry ingredients.

3. Set the bread machine to the gluten-free setting.

4. When the bread is done, remove the bread machine pan from the bread machine. 5.Let cool slightly before transferring to a cooling rack.

6.You can store your bread for up to 5 days.

Nutrition: Calories: 132 Carbohydrates: 4g Protein: 6g Fat: 8 g

Cheesy Garlic Bread

Preparation Time: 30 minutes **Cooking Time**: 15 minutes **Serving**: 10

Ingredients:

- cup mozzarella, shredded
- cup almond flour
- tbsps. cream cheese
- tbsp. garlic, crushed
- tbsp. parsley
- tsp baking powder
- Salt, to taste
- egg

For the toppings:

- tbsps. melted butter
- tsp parsley
- tsp garlic clove, minced

Directions:

1. Mix your topping ingredients and set them aside.

2. Pour the remaining wet ingredients into the bread machine pan.

3. Add the dry ingredients.

4. Set the bread machine to the gluten-free setting.

5. When the bread is done, remove the bread machine pan from the bread machine.

6. Let cool slightly before transferring to a cooling rack.

7.Once on a cooling rack, drizzle with the topping mix.

8. You can store your bread for up to 7 days.

Nutrition: Calories: 29 Carbohydrates: 1g Protein: 2g Fiber 1g Fat: 2g

Bacon Jalapeño Cheesy Bread

Preparation Time: 22 minutes **Cooking Time**: 15 minutes **Serving**: 12

Ingredients:

- cup golden flaxseed, ground
- cup coconut flour
- tsp baking powder
- tsp black peppertbsp. erythritol
- 1/3 cup pickled jalapeno
- oz. cream cheese, full fat
- eggs
- cups sharp cheddar cheese, shredded + ¼ cup extra for the topping
- tbsps. parmesan cheese, grated
- ¼ cup almond milk
- Bacon Slices (cooked and crumbled)
- cup rendered bacon grease (from frying the bacon)
- **Directions:**

1.   Cook the bacon in a larger frying pan, set it aside to cool on paper towels. Save ¼ cup of bacon fat for the recipe, allow to cool slightly before using.

2.   Add wet ingredients to bread machine pan, including the cooled bacon grease. 3.Add in the remaining ingredients.

4.   Set the bread machine to the quick bread setting.

5.   When the bread is done, remove the bread machine pan from the bread machine.

6. Let cool slightly before transferring to a cooling rack.

7.   Once on a cooling rack, top with the remaining cheddar cheese.8. You can store your bread for up to 7 days. **Nutrition**: Calories: 235 Carbohydrates: 5g Protein: 11g Fat: 17g

Cheddar Herb Bread

Preparation Time :10

Cooking Time: 15

Serving: 16

Ingredients:

- cup butter, room temperature
- eggs
- tsp baking powder
- cups almond flour
- tsp xanthan gum
- ½ cups cheddar cheese, shredded
- tbsp. garlic powder
- tbsp. parsley
- tbsp. oregano

Directions:

1. Lightly beat eggs and butter together then add to the bread machine pan. 2.Add dry ingredients to the pan.

3. Set the bread to the gluten free setting.

4. When the bread is done, remove the bread machine pan from the bread machine. 5.Let cool slightly before transferring to a cooling rack.

6.You can store your bread for up to 5 days.

Nutrition:

Calories: 142 Carbohydrates: 3g Protein: 6g

Fat: 13g

Faux Sourdough Bread

Preparation Time: 10 minutes **Cooking Time**: 15

Servings: 12

Ingredients:

- cups bread flour (white)
- cup plus 1 tablespoon hot water
- cup sour cream
- 1½ tablespoons butter, melted
- tablespoon apple cider vinegar
- tablespoon sugar
- teaspoon salt
- teaspoon instant yeast

Directions:

1.Put all ingredients in the bread machine. 2.Set the bread machine to French bread.

3.When ready, remove the bread and allow about 5 minutes to cool the loaf. 4. Put it on a rack to cool it completely

Nutrition:

Calories: 102 Carbohydrates: 2.5g Fat: 4g Protein: 4g Fiber: 1g

Cranberry Bread

Preparation Time: 10 minutes **Cooking Time**: 15 minutes **Serving**: 20

Ingredients:

- cups almond flour
- cup erythritol
- ½ tsp baking powder
- tsp baking soda
- tsp salt
- tbsps. coconut oil
- tsp nutmeg, ground
- eggs
- cup coconut milk
- 12 Oz cranberries

Directions:

1.Add wet ingredients to the bread machine pan.

2.Add dry ingredients to the bread machine pan.

3.Set bread machine to the gluten-free setting.

4.   When it is ready, remove the pan from the machine.

5.   Let cool slightly before transferring to a cooling rack. 6.You can store your bread for up to 5 days.

Nutrition:

Calories: 127

Carbohydrates: 10g

Protein: 3g

Fat: 11g

Basil Cheese Bread

Preparation time: 5 minutes **Cooking time**: 15 minutes **Servings**: 10

Ingredients:

- Almond flour, two cups
- Warm water, one cup
- Salt, half a teaspoon
- Basil dried, one teaspoon
- Half cup of mozzarella shredded cheese
- Quarter tsp. Of active dry yeast
- tsp. Of melted unsalted butter
- tsp. Of stevia powder

Directions:

1.   In a mixing container, combine the almond flour, dried basil, salt, shredded mozzarella cheese, and stevia powder.

2.   Get another container, where you will combine the warm water and the melted unsalted butter.

3.   As per the instructions on the manual of your machine, pour the ingredients in the bread pan, taking care to follow how to mix in the yeast.

4.   Place the bread pan in the machine, and select the sweet bread setting, together with the crust type, if available, then press start once you have closed the lid of the machine.

5.   When the bread is ready, using oven mitts, remove the bread pan from the machine. Use a stainless spatula to extract the bread from the pan and turn the pan upside down on a metallic rack where the bread will cool off before slicing it.

Nutrition:

Calories: 124 Fat: 8g Carb: 2g Protein: 11g

American Cheese Beer Bread

Preparation time: 5 minutes **Cooking time**: 15 minutes **Servings**: 10

Ingredients:

- ½ cups of fine almond flour
- tsp. Of unsalted melted butter
- Salt, one teaspoon
- An egg
- Swerve sweetener, two teaspoons
- Keto low-Carb beer, one cup
- tsp. Of baking powder
- cup of cheddar cheese, shredded
- tsp. Of active dry yeast

Directions:

1.   Prepare a mixing container, where you will combine the almond flour, swerve sweetener, salt, shredded cheddar cheese, and baking powder.

2.   Prepare another mixing container, where you will combine the unsalted melted butter, egg, and low-Carb keto beer.

3.   As per the instructions on the manual of your machine, pour the ingredients in the bread pan, taking care to follow how to mix in the yeast.

4.   Place the bread pan in the machine, and select the basic bread setting, together with the bread size and crust type, if available, then press start once you have closed the lid of the machine.

5.   When the bread is ready, using oven mitts, remove the bread pan from the machine. Use a stainless spatula to extract the bread from the pan and turn the pan upside down on a metallic rack where the bread will cool off before slicing it.

Nutrition:

Calories: 94 Fat: 6g Carb: 4g Protein: 1g

Parmesan Cheddar Bread

Preparation time: 5 minutes

Cooking time: 15 minutes

Servings: 10

Ingredients:

Parmesan cheese grated, one cup

Almond flour, one cup

Baking powder, half a teaspoon

Salt, 3/4 teaspoon

Cayenne pepper, a quarter teaspoon

Unsweetened almond milk half a cup

Sour cream, a third cup full

Active dry yeast, one teaspoon

tsp. Of unsalted melted butter

egg

Directions:

1.   Get a container for mixing, and combine the almond flour, shredded parmesan cheese, cayenne pepper, baking powder, and salt.

2.   In another mixing container, combine the unsweetened almond milk, sour cream, egg, and un-salted melted butter.

3.　As per the instructions on the manual of your machine, pour the ingredients in the bread pan, taking care to follow how to mix in the yeast.

4.　Place the bread pan in the machine, and select the basic bread setting, together with the bread size and crust type, if available, then press start once you have closed the lid of the machine.

5.　When the bread is ready, using oven mitts, remove the bread pan from the machine. Use a stainless spatula to extract the bread from the pan and turn the pan upside down on a metallic rack where the bread will cool off before slicing it.

Nutrition:

Calories: 134 Fat: 6.8g Carb: 4.2g Protein: 12.1g

Pepper Cheddar Bread

Preparation time: 5 minutes **Cooking time**: 15 minutes **Servings**: 10

Ingredients:

Cup of coconut flour

Cup of almond blanched fine flour

Tsp. Of black pepper powder

Cup of warm water

Cheese of cheddar grated, one cup

Salt, one teaspoon

Unsalted melted butter, two teaspoons

Baking powder, one teaspoon

Active dry yeast, one tea-spoon

Directions:

1.   Get a container for mixing, and combine the almond flour, coconut flour, shredded cheddar cheese, black pepper powder, baking powder, and salt.

2.   Get another container, where you will combine the warm water and unsalted melted butter.

3.   As per the instructions on the manual of your machine, pour the ingredients in the bread pan, taking care to follow how to mix in the yeast.

4.   Place the bread pan in the machine, and select the basic bread setting, together with the bread size and crust type, if available, then press start once you have closed the lid of the machine.

5.   When the bread is ready, using oven mitts, remove the bread pan from the machine.

6.   Use a stainless spatula to extract the bread from the pan and turn the pan upside down on a metallic rack where the bread will cool off before slicing it.

Nutrition:

Calories: 84 Fat: 4g Carb: 3g Protein: 1g

Olive Cheese Bread

Preparation time: 5 minutes **Cooking time**: 15 minute: **Servings:** 10

Ingredients:

Almond flour, one cup

- Coconut flour, a third cup full
- Olives black halved, a full cup
- Olives green halved, a full cup
- Baking powder, one teaspoon
- Active dry yeast, one teaspoon
- Almond milk, unsweetened, a third cup full
- Shredded mozzarella cheese, two-thirds of a cup
- cup of melted unsalted butter
- cup of chopped green onions
- 1/3 cup of mayon-naise

Directions:

1.   In a mixing container, combine the almond flour, coconut flour, shredded mozzarella cheese, chopped green onions, chopped black olives, chopped green olives, and baking powder.

2.   Prepare another mixing container, where you will combine the unsweetened almond milk, mayonnaise, and melted unsalted butter.

3.   As per the instructions on the manual of your machine, pour the ingredients in the bread pan, taking care to follow how to mix in the yeast.

4.   Place the bread pan in the machine, and select the basic bread setting, together with the bread size and crust type, if available, then press start once you have closed the lid of the machine.

5.   When the bread is ready, extract it, and place it on a metallic mesh surface to cool completely before cutting and eating it.

Nutrition:

Calories: 134 Fat: 6.8g Carb: 4.2g Protein: 12.1g

Feta Oregano Bread

Preparation time: 5 minutes

Cooking time: 15 minutes

Servings: 10

Ingredients:

- Almond flour, one cup
- Crumbled feta cheese, one cup
- Half cup of warm water
- Oregano dried, one teaspoon
- Baking powder, two-thirds of a teaspoon
- Extra virgin olive oil, a teaspoon
- Salt, half a teaspoon
- Swerve sweetener, one teaspoon
- Garlic powder, a quarter teaspoon
- Dried active yeast, one tea-spoon

Directions:

1.   In a mixing container, combine the almond flour, swerve sweetener, dried oregano, baking powder, ground garlic, and salt.

2.   In another mixing container, combine the extra virgin olive oil and warm water.

3.   As per the instructions on the manual of your machine, pour the ingredients in the bread pan, taking care to follow how to mix in the yeast.

4.   Place the bread pan in the machine, and select the sweet bread setting, together with the bread size and crust type, if available, then press start once you have closed the lid of the machine.

5.   When the bread is ready, using oven mitts, remove the bread pan from the machine. Use a stainless spatula to extract the bread from the pan and turn the pan upside down on a metallic rack where the bread will cool off before slicing it.

Nutrition:

Calories: 114 Fat: 7g Carb: 8g Protein: 9g

Goat Cheese Bread

Preparation time: 5 minutes

Cooking time: 15 minutes

Servings: 10

Ingredients:

- cup of almond blanched fine flour
- cup of soy flour
- of salt
- tsp. Of fresh thyme, crushed
- cup of coconut milk, melted
- tsp. Of pepper cayenne
- Eggs, two
- Mustard of dijon, one teaspoon
- Crumbled fresh goat cheese, one cup
- Baking powder, one teaspoon
- Olive oil, extra virgin, a third cup full
- Active dry yeast, one tea-spoon

Directions:

1.   Get a mixing container an
d combine the almond flour, soy flour, fresh thyme, cayenne pepper, salt, crumbled fresh goat cheese, and baking powder.

2.   Get another mixing container and combine extra virgin olive oil, eggs, coconut milk, and dijon mustard.

3.   As per the instructions on the manual of your machine, pour the ingredients in the bread pan, taking care to follow how to mix in the yeast.

4.   Place the bread pan in the machine, and select the basic bread setting, together with the bread size and crust type, if available, then press start once you have closed the lid of the machine.

5.   When the bread is ready, using oven mitts, remove the bread pan from the machine. Use a stain-less spatula to extract the bread from the pan and turn the pan upside down on a metallic rack where the bread will cool off before slicing it.

Nutrition:

Calories: 134

Fat: 6.8g Carb: 4.2g Protein: 12.1g

Mozzarella Herbs Bread

Preparation time: 5 minutes

Cooking time: 15 minutes **Servings**: 10

Ingredients:

- Grated cheese mozzarella, one cup
- Grated cheese parmesan, half a cup
- Salt, half a teaspoon
- Baking powder, one teaspoon
- Almond flour, one cup
- Coconut flour, one cup
- Warm water, half a cup
- Stevia, one teaspoon
- Thyme, dried, a quarter teaspoon
- Garlic, ground, one teaspoon
- Basil, dried, one teaspoon
- Olive oil, extra virgin, one teaspoon
- Unsalted melted butter, two teaspoons
- third cup of unsweetened almond milk

Directions:

1.   In a mixing container, mix the almond flour, baking powder, salt, parmesan cheese, mozzarella cheese, coconut flour, dried basil, dried thyme, garlic powder, and stevia powder.

2.   Get another mixing container and mix warm water, unsweetened almond milk, melted unsalted butter, and extra virgin olive oil.

3.   As per the instructions on the manual of your machine, pour the ingredients in the bread pan, taking care to follow how to mix in the yeast.

4.   Place the bread pan in the machine, and select the basic bread setting, together with the bread size and crust type, if available, then press start once you have closed the lid of the machine.

5.   When the bread is ready, using oven mitts, remove the bread pan from the machine. Use a stainless spatula to extract the bread from the pan and turn the pan upside down on a metallic rack where the bread will cool off before slicing it.

Nutrition:

Calories: 49 Fat: 2g Carb: 2g Protein: 1g

Blue Cheese Onion Bread

Preparation time: 5 minutes **Cooking time**: 15 minutes **Servings**: 10

Ingredients:

- Half a cup of blue cheese, crumbled
- tsp. Of unsalted melted butter
- tsp. Of fresh rosemary, chopped
- ½ cup of almond fine flour
- Olive oil extra virgin, two teaspoons
- Baking powder, one teaspoon
- Warm water, half a cup
- yellow onion sliced and sautéed in butter until golden brown
- garlic cloves, crushed
- Yeast, one teaspoon
- Swerve sweetener, one teaspoon
- Salt, one teaspoon

Directions:

1. Prepare a mix
2. ing container, where you will combine the almond flour, swerve sweetener, bak-ing powder, freshly chopped rosemary, crumbled

blue cheese, sautéed sliced onion, salt, and crushed garlic.

2. Get another container, where you will combine the warm water, melted butter, and extra virgin olive oil.

3. As per the instructions on the manual of your machine, pour the ingredients in the bread pan, taking care to follow how to mix in the yeast.

4. Place the bread pan in the machine, and select the basic bread setting, together with the bread size and crust type, if available, then press start once you have closed the lid of the machine.

5. When the bread is ready, using oven mitts, remove the bread pan from the machine. Use a stainless spatula to extract the bread from the pan, and turn the pan upside down on a metallic rack where the bread will cool off before slicing it.

Nutrition:

Calories: 100 Fat: 6g Carb: 3g Protein: 11g

CPSIA information can be obtained
at www.ICGtesting.com
Printed in the USA
BVHW091434030521
606339BV00006B/845